Pen in Hand:
a journal

by Katie Proctor

copyright 2021 Katie Proctor

Dear readers (and writers!),

In <u>Hand in Hand</u>, Hazel and Lily find that even though they are such different people, they find common ground in the books they read. Also, the girls find that a great way to communicate their thoughts and feelings about the books they read is through writing back and forth in their journal. As we learn from Hazel and Lily, words really matter. They have the power to break down or build up. I hope that you will use this journal to pay attention to the world, your place in it, and how you can use your words for good. The questions are designed to get you thinking critically about a variety of topics, and also to have a bit of fun!

There are a few questions in this journal that connect writing and reading. Reading becomes such a deeper experience when we write about what we read in books. Maybe these are lessons you learn from important characters, examining the feelings that a really good book can bring up in you, thinking about people in your life who might like a certain book as much as you do. Brain scientists tell us that writing can be an important tool in processing feelings and also that we are wired for connection. Reading and writing can both be great ways to bring people together.

These pages can be just for you, a place to record your secrets and thoughts, or it can be shared with whoever you trust with your words. However you use it, my hope is that it helps your creativity come alive and that you experiment with language and take risks in your writing. And just remember, your words matter.

Much love and inspiration to you,

Katie Proctor

One of the things Hazel and Lily love the most is reading. How do you feel about reading?

Do you have a favorite book? What makes it special to you?

Who got you interested in reading? Maybe a parent? Or teacher? Sibling? Friend? Tell about them here.

Just like Lily and Hazel do, use these next couple of pages to write about the books you're reading. What do they make you think? Feel? Wonder about?

....

....

....

....

....

....

....

....

....

....

....

....

....

....

....

....

Do you think people can read too much? Why or why not?

Choose a favorite character from a book and write them a letter--OR--Write a letter to a favorite author (and then send them a copy! They'd love it, I promise!)

What section(s) of the library or bookstore do you like to visit the most? Circle all that apply!

Fiction   Nonfiction

Graphic novels   Picture books

                Chapter books

What kind of books do you usually grab off the shelves?

....

....

Let's do your own little reading challenge! Write the title and give yourself a sticker or check off each category you complete!

Reread a favorite picture book	A mystery
Listen to an audiobook (or have someone read to you!)	Build a comfy book fort and read a book in it
A book that was published the year you were born	A fantasy book

A historical fiction book	A book of poems ....
Read a book outside	A book from a favorite author or series ....
A classic (try one of the ones in <u>Hand in Hand</u>!)	A book recommended by friend or family member ....
A graphic novel	A nonfiction book about a topic that interests you ....
A book set in a really far away place	A book that was made into a movie ....

How does it make you feel to read about hard things, like the way Mr. Adams treated Hazel? Why do you think it might be important to read about things like this?

Why do you think we need to read stories about history? What can we learn from them?

Let s talk about your friends. What makes them great friends? What do you like doing with them?

Have you ever gotten into an argument with a good friend? What was it about? How did you resolve it?

Tell about a time you had to apologize to someone. How did it feel?

Write about a time you saw someone (in real life, or in books or TV or movie) be treated in a hateful way for who they are. How did it make you feel? How do you think the person being treated badly felt?

....

....

....

....

....

....

....

....

....

....

....

....

....

....

....

What do you know about racism and prejudice in history? What do you know about racism and prejudice in today's world?

Did any of the events in <u>Hand in Hand</u> surprise you? Why or why not?

Tell a family story like "Alice the Ghost." These are stories your family might tell over and over. If you can't think of one, find an older adult who can tell you a fun story and write it here.

Do you have siblings? (If not, think about cousins or close friends for this one). How do you get along with them? Do you always agree with them? What happens when you don't?

Miss Grace is such an amazing teacher to Hazel. Tell about a favorite teacher here. What makes them so special?

There is a lot of traditional Southern food in <u>Hand in Hand</u>. What are some traditional foods you and your family enjoy together?

Write about a food you love to cook (or help cook). Who taught you how to make it? Share the recipe and instructions here or a special memory about making it. If you can't think of anything specifically, invent a dream food you'd love to cook someday.

Superheroes might not exist in our world, but write about ways you see people being heroes around you in ordinary ways.

If you could time travel back in history to any place and time, where would you go and what would you want to do there?

Tell about a time (or make up a pretend story) when you were really scared (like Lily was in the fire or Hazel when her brother was sick).

If your town was small like Mayfield and you could go anywhere on your bike, where would you go and what would you do?

Choose a time and place in history you want to learn more about. Do some research (library books, internet with adult help, educational TV or documentary) to find out more about it. Use this guide to help you take notes.

When? What is the time period you're researching?	
Who? Who were some important people alive at the time?	
What? What interesting things happened during this time? What was the technology like? How did people do basic things like get food, travel, and communicate with others?	

Where? Describe the place you've chosen to research. What does it look like? What would it feel like to be there?	
Why? Why is this time period important to you? What makes it stand out?	

Create a character who would live in this time. Tell what they look like, act like, think about, how they talk, who they know, what they like to do.

Think of a few problems that your character might face and how they might solve them. Keep in mind that depending on the time you've chosen they might not have the technology that we do.

Problem	Solution

Write an imaginary story using details from your research and your character's problems and solutions.

Thank you for writing with us! For more reads and writes, join us at
www.FawkesPress.com/newsletter

If you would like to share your work, have an adult upload a picture and tag us on Instagram @katieproctorwritesandreads and @fawkespress You may also e-mail a picture to katieproctorwrites@gmail.com

We'd love to see your work because

YOU MATTER!

www.ingramcontent.com/pod-product-compliance
Lightning Source LLC
Chambersburg PA
CBHW030141100526
44592CB00011B/999